Growing Up a Country Girl

Flowers
and Fields
and Fun
in the Sun

Paintings by
Donald Zolan

HARVEST HOUSE PUBLISHERS

EUGENE, OREGON

Growing Up a Country Girl

Text Copyright © 2005 by Harvest House Publishers
Eugene, Oregon 97402
www.harvesthousepublishers.com

ISBN-13: 978-0-7369-1368-3
ISBN-10: 0-7369-1368-8

Zolan Fine Arts, LLC
Attn: Jennifer Zolan
70 Blackman Road
Ridgefield, CT 06877
203.431.1629
www.zolan.com

Design and production by Garborg Design Works, Minneapolis, Minnesota

Printed in Hong Kong

08 09 10 11 / NG / 10 9 8 7 6

A country life is sweet!
In moderate cold and heat,
To walk in the air, how pleasant and fair!
In every field of wheat,
The fairest of the flowers adorning the bowers
And every meadow's brow;
So that I say, no courier may
Compare with them who clothe in gray,
And follow the useful plow.

They rise with the morning lark,
And labor till almost dark;
Then, folding their sheep, they hasten to sleep,
While every pleasant park
Next morning is ringing with birds that are singing
On each green, tender bough.
With what content and merriment
Their days are spent, whose minds are bent
To follow the useful plow.

AUTHOR UNKNOWN

In her opinion having to depend upon one's self to decide courses of action as much as you do in farm life, gives one back-bone and trains one to rely upon self and to be an effective leader. She has, as most true country people have, an ineradicable and fundamental passion for independence.

MARTHA FOOTE CROW
The American Country Girl

Elizabeth made a vivid picture as she ran down the path between two straight rows of young orchard trees to the spring in the south meadow, swinging a large wooden pail in either hand. The noon sun made her brown hair bronze and brought out the deep flush of excitement in her face. She was singing broken bits of the only gay song her Puritan ears had ever heard...So a very gay little maid set her pails where the clear water from the spring could filter into them and smiled happily at the familiar landscape. To the south of the big meadow lay the cornfields. The stalks, swaying heavily beneath loads of filled out ears, parted enough to show hundreds of fat yellow pumpkins.

GERTRUDE ROBINSON
"A Girl of Maine"
New England Magazine, 1904

The care of the ranch fell upon the daughters, Miss Gussie, and Miss Louise, Lahm. These young women now, therefore, devote their time to the practical affairs of stock-raising, and the varied details of a mountain farm. Their five thousand sheep, together with droves of horses and cattle, look to them for care. They brand the increase of the sheep, supervise the shearing and market the wool. Plowing, harrowing, sowing and harvesting are in the list of their agricultural employments. Tracking, trapping, and shooting game are their avocations. The reatas at their saddles are used by hands that can lasso a wild horse or a steer with unerring success. In the late fall months, when the grass is short, the stock are fed in the corrals, but at other times they stray and must be driven in at night. It may not be the idyllic picture of the traditional pastoral heroine, but it is, none the less, a pleasing one to see the great flock of silly sheep and bleating lambs running before their modern herders and their dogs. Your shepherdess of song and fable is a lovely little fairy with a ribboned crook. With yawning difference, these modern Californian ones have guns and lariats and are clad in the Amazonian garb of overalls and jumpers.

W. F. WADE
"The Girl-Ranchers of California"
The Cosmopolitan, 1900

Girls especially are fond of exchanging confidences with those whom they think they can trust; it is one of the most charming traits of a simple, earnest-hearted girlhood.

LUCY LARCOM

Perhaps my next remedy shall be a revival of a calm, true love of nature. Our athletic advances have thrust themselves between us and nature's greatest charm. No thought of breaking records or of winning matches must intrude upon the silence of the nature-lover.

HELOISE EDWINA HERSEY
"The Amusements of Girls"
The Independent, 1901

9

"Farm life to me is attractive," she says, *"because on the farm one has the freedom that cannot be gained anywhere else in the world. One learns the habits of birds and animals and comes in touch with nature and hence with the Creator himself."*

MARTHA FOOTE CROW
The American Country Girl

We knew that we lived on the summit of the world because the sky was tallest above our chimneys...We were little candles in pinafores set upon a hill to shine. And we were ready to magnify the illuminating dignity of our calling. For if we were less than godly, at least we were spiritually minded. And by putting all things together after the exaggerated manner of young children—we were blessed with the presumption that we had been set apart by heaven for some great purpose, which would be revealed to us...But for all our prayers and expectations, no burning bush ever appeared in our childish by-ways. We were only two little tadpole saints, without a grief or a care to try our spirits.

AUTHOR UNKNOWN
"Memories of an Early Girlhood"
The Independent, 1903

Put a bit of sunshine in the day;
Others need its cheer and so do you—
Need it most when outer sky's dull gray
Leaves the sunshine-making yours to do.

Give the day a streak of rosy dawn;
Give it, too, a touch of highest noon;
Make the ones about you wonder why
Sunset crimson should appear "so soon."

Sunshine-making is a blessed task;
Cheery hearts, like lovely wide-blue sky,
Banish weary gloom and give fresh hope,
Check the rising tear or thoughtless sigh.

Put the golden sunshine in each day;
Others need the cheer that comes through you—
Need it most when outer sky's dull gray
Leaves the sunshine-making yours to do.

Juniata Stafford
"Scatter Sunshine"

13

Nothing rounder, slenderer, or more richly tinted was ever cast into the feminine mold. A perfect creature, modeled after approved patterns, which English speaking nations have been copying closely for generations. The salient points which go to make up the beauty of an American girl are a general delicacy of outline, as well as of coloring, a face molded in delicate lines and features that are thoroughly harmonious.

AUTHOR UNKNOWN
"The Typical American Girl"
The Brooklyn Eagle, 1902

Little girls are the nicest things that happen to people.

ALAN BECK

Miss Lucreece was busy among her roses. Tall old bushes laden with bloom, lined either side of the brick walk, which led up to her small white house, and here and there between these fragrant veterans, low tea-rose clusters peered out and offered their small sweet wares. They were old friends, Miss Lucreece and the roses. When she was a little girl, their tallest sprays had hung just a span's breadth above the golden glint of her dark curls, and they still nodded just a span's breadth over the locks whose golden glint had long since softened into a silver shimmer.

EDITH RICHMOND BLANCHARD
"When the Rose Bloomed"
New England Magazine, March 1904

All our days are not so busy...and when the haying and summer sewing are done, we have a chance for good times. Our haying was done this summer in eight days or perhaps less. At quarter of nine we go to bed. I read a chapter or two in some book I am reading, but by ten o'clock we are both asleep with the starlight and the moonlight shining in on us through the open screen.

MARTHA FOOTE CROWE
The American Country Girl

The world beyond the orchard was in a royal magnificence of colouring, under the vivid blue autumn sky. The big willow by the gate was a splendid golden dome, and the maples that were scattered through the spruce grove waved blood-red banners over the sombre cone-bearers. The Story Girl generally had her head garlanded with their leaves. They became her vastly. Neither Felicity nor Cecily could have worn them. Those two girls were of a domestic type that assorted ill with the wildfire in Nature's veins. But when the Story Girl wreathed her nut brown tresses with crimson leaves it seemed, as Peter said, that they grew on her—as if the gold and flame of her spirit had broken out in a coronal...

LUCY M. MONTGOMERY
The Story Girl

18

I love the taste of thorn apples and sweet acorns and sumac and
  choke-cherries and all the wild things we used to find on
  the road to school.
And I love the feel of pussy willows and the inside of chestnut
  burrs.
I love to walk on a country road where only a few double teams
  have left a strip of turf in the middle of the track.

20

And I love the creaking of the sleigh runners and the snapping
 of nail-heads in the clapboards on a bitter cold January night.
In the first cool nights I love the sound of the first hard rainfall on
 the roof of the gable room.

And I love the smell of the dead leaves in the woods in the fall.
I love the odor of those red apples that grew on the trees that
 died before I went back to grandpa's again.
I love the fragrance of the first pink and blue hepaticas which
 have hardly any scent at all.
I love the smell of the big summer raindrops on the dusty dry steps
 of the school house.
I love the breath of the great corn fields when you ride past them
 on an August evening in the dark.

And I love to see the wind blowing over tall grass.
I love the yellow afternoon light that turns all the trees and shrubs
 to gold.
I love to see the shadow of a cloud moving over the valley,
 especially where the different fields have different colors
 like a great checkerboard.
I love the little ford over Turtle Creek where they didn't build the
 bridge after the freshet.
I love the sunset on the hill in Winnebago County, where I used to
 sit and pray about my mental arithmetic lesson the spring
 I taught school!

ELIZABETH WILSON

But I was hearty and robust, full of frolicsome health, and very fond of the matter-of-fact world I lived in. My sturdy little feet felt the solid earth beneath them. I grew with the sprouting grass, and enjoyed my life as the buds and birds seemed to enjoy theirs. It was only as if the bud and the bird and the dear warm earth knew, in the same dumb way that I did, that all their joy and sweetness came to them out of the sky.

Lucy Larcom

I think that as a rule we display more energy, even if we do not accomplish much, during the first six years of life than we ever do again in the same length of time. It is the experimental period, when we are engaged in testing the impossibilities of everything about us. Certainly these were the most enterprising years of my own existence.

Author Unknown
"Memories of an Early Girlhood"
The Independent, 1903

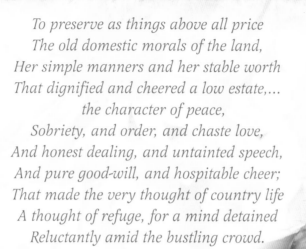

To preserve as things above all price
The old domestic morals of the land,
Her simple manners and her stable worth
That dignified and cheered a low estate,...
the character of peace,
Sobriety, and order, and chaste love,
And honest dealing, and untainted speech,
And pure good-will, and hospitable cheer;
That made the very thought of country life
A thought of refuge, for a mind detained
Reluctantly amid the bustling crowd.

WILLIAM WORDSWORTH

After supper again I saddled Daisy and went for the cows while my sisters washed the supper dishes. That evening as we gathered around the kitchen table and my father read a chapter from the Bible, I think I was one of the happiest girls in the world even if I was tired. As I went to bed that evening I thanked the dear Father that I had a father, mother, brothers, and sisters to love and help care for.

MARTHA FOOTE CROW
The American Country Girl

25

The girl that can in the midst of her rigid daily duties fall on her knees and thank God for the dim, black forests which are the eternal fans of nature, for the rain that appeases the thirst of the birds of the air, and the newly sown seed in the fields, that can feel amid these natural objects awe, admiration, a sense of infinite force, of boundless life, of duration that is eternal in its broad and human sweep, leaving her stunned with the realization of her pygmied self in the presence of these veritable facts, and at the same time filling her with a deep pride that she, too, is a living, necessary factor in God's world of Rural Life is the one that possesses the power to rise above the common drudgeries of daily existence. She knows the secret of the beautiful and simple life is to make oneself a symbol of heavenly life.

SIGISMUND VON EBERSTADT

That which caused us the liveliest apprehension was the varying shapes of the clouds. Never did a huge headed cloud shake its misty beard at us that we did not drop everything in a panic and fly for shelter. Once, just after listening to a tale about polar bears, we saw an immense white Juggernaut monster roll up over our horizon. Clasping hands, we ran toward the house as fast as our little terror-shaken legs could carry us. But when we reached the calm door sill of our castle we told no one of our narrow escape. Personally we never doubted that we had escaped a most frightful end, but we dreaded lest the idea might seem absurd to our elders.

AUTHOR UNKNOWN
"Memories of an Early Girlhood"
The Independent, 1903

It is such fun to visit the other girls, to taste their goodies,
to sleep four in a bed, toast marshmallows, and make fudge.

MARTHA FOOTE CROW

The Law of the Camp Fire

—Seek beauty
—Give service
—Pursue knowledge
—Be trustworthy
—Hold on to health
—Glorify work
—Be happy

Camp Fire Girls Handbook, 1914

We much preferred to sit on the sunken curbstones, in the shade of the broad-leaved burdocks, and shape their spiny balls into chairs and cradles and sofas for our dollies, or to "play school" on the doorsteps, or to climb over the wall, and to feel the freedom of the hill.

LUCY LARCOM

Anne dropped on her knees and gazed out into the June morning, her eyes glistening with delight. Oh, wasn't it beautiful? Wasn't it a lovely place? Suppose she wasn't really going to stay here! She would imagine she was. There was scope for imagination here.

A huge cherry-tree grew outside, so close that its boughs tapped against the house, and it was so thick-set with blossoms that hardly a leaf was to be seen. On both sides of the house was a big orchard, one of apple-trees and one of cherry-trees, also showered over with blossoms; and their grass was all sprinkled with dandelions. In the garden below were lilac-trees purple with flowers, and their dizzily sweet fragrance drifted up to the window on the morning wind.

Below the garden a green field lush with clover sloped down to the hollow where the brook ran and where scores of white birches grew, upspringing airily out of an undergrowth suggestive of delightful possibilities in ferns and mosses and woodsy things generally. Beyond it was a hill, green and feathery with spruce and fir; there was a gap in it where the gray gable end of the little house she had seen from the other side of the Lake of Shining Waters was visible.

Off to the left were the big barns and beyond them, away down over green, low-sloping fields, was a sparkling blue glimpse of sea.

Anne's beauty-loving eyes lingered on it all, taking everything greedily in. She had looked on so many unlovely places in her life, poor child; but this was as lovely as anything she had ever dreamed.

Lucy M. Montgomery
Anne of Green Gables

*These were the winding ways up our
castle-towers, with breakfast-rooms and boudoirs
along the landings, where we set our tables for
expected guests with bits of broken china, and left
our numerous rag-children tucked in asleep under
mullein blankets or plantain-coverlets, while we
ascended to the topmost turret to watch for our
ships coming in from sea.*

LUCY LARCOM

She started joyfully for the mountain. During the night the wind had blown away all the clouds; the dark blue sky was spreading overhead, and in its midst was the bright sun shining down on the green slopes of the mountain, where the flowers opened their little blue and yellow cups, and looked up to him smiling. Heidi went running hither and thither and shouting with delight, for here were whole patches of delicate red primroses, and there the blue gleam of the lovely gentian, while above them all laughed and nodded the tender-leaved golden cistus. Enchanted with all this waving field of brightly colored flowers, Heidi forgot even Peter and the goats. She ran on in front and then off to the side, tempted first one way and then the other, as she caught sight of some bright spot of glowing red or yellow. And all the while she was plucking whole handfuls of the flowers which she put into her little apron, for she wanted to take them all home and stick them in the hay, so that she might make her bedroom look just like the meadows outside.

JOHANNA SPYRI
Heidi

A girl is Innocence playing in the mud, Beauty standing on its head,
and Motherhood dragging a doll by the foot.

ALAN BECK

"What in the world are you going to do now, Jo?" asked Meg one snowy afternoon, as her sister came tramping through the hall, in rubber boots, old sack, and hood, with a broom in one hand and a shovel in the other.

"Going out for exercise," answered Jo with a mischievous twinkle in her eyes.

"I should think two long walks this morning would have been enough! It's cold and dull out, and I advise you to stay warm and dry by the fire, as I do," said Meg with a shiver.

"Never take advice! Can't keep still all day, and not being a pussycat, I don't like to doze by the fire. I like adventures, and I'm going to find some."

Meg went back to toast her feet and read *Ivanhoe,* and Jo began to dig paths with great energy. The snow was light, and with her broom she soon swept a path all round the garden, for Beth to walk in when the sun came out and the invalid dolls needed air.

LOUISA MAY ALCOTT
Little Women

It is especially important that whatever will prepare country children for life on the farm, and whatever will brighten home life in the country and make it richer and more attractive for the mothers, wives, and daughters of farmers should be done promptly, thoroughly, and gladly. There is no more important person, measured in great influence upon the life of the nation, than the farmer's wife, no more important home than the country home, and it is of national importance to do the best we can for both.

THEODORE ROOSEVELT

At first the road lay between fertile farms dotted with shocked wheat, covered with undulant seas of ripening oats, and forests of growing corn. The larks were trailing melody above the shorn and growing fields, the quail were ingathering beside the fences, and from the forests on graceful wings slipped the nighthawks and sailed and soared, dropping so low that the half moons formed by white spots on their spread wings showed plainly.

"Why is this country so different from the other side of the city?" asked the Girl.

"It is older," replied the Harvester, "and it lies higher. This was settled and well cultivated when that was a swamp. But as a farming proposition, the money is in the lowland like your uncle's. The crops raised there are enormous compared with the yield of these fields."

GENE STRATTON-PORTER
The Harvester

The stars brought me the same feeling. I remember the surprise they were to me, seen for the first time. One evening, just before I was put to bed, I was taken in somebody's arms—my sister's, I think—outside the door, and lifted up under the dark, still, clear sky, splendid with stars, thicker and nearer earth than they have ever seemed since. All my little being shaped itself into a subdued delighted "Oh!" And then the exultant thought flitted through the mind of the reluctant child, as she was carried in, "Why, that is the roof of the house I live in." After that I always went to sleep happier for the feeling that the stars were outside there in the dark, though I could not see them.

LUCY LARCOM

The girl looked at them without thinking, and then she raised her eyes and was almost dazzled at the sight of the apple trees in blossom. Just then a colt, full of life and friskiness, jumped over the ditches and then stopped suddenly, as if surprised at being alone.

She also felt inclined to run; she felt inclined to move and to stretch her limbs and to repose in the warm, breathless air. She took a few undecided steps and closed her eyes, for she was seized with a feeling of animal comfort, and then she went to look for eggs in the hen loft.

GUY DE MAUPASSANT
The Story of a Farm Girl

39

Little Lucy was that
rather rare creature,
a very gentle, obedient
child, with a single
eye for her duty. She
was so charming.

MARY E. WILKINS FREEMAN
Little Lucy Rose

'Tis true, your budding miss is very charming,
But shy and awkward at first coming out,
So much alarm's, that she is quite alarming,
All Giggle, Blush; half Pertness, and half Pout;
And glancing at Mamma, for fear there's harm in
What you, she, it, or they, may be about,
The nursery still lisps out in all they utter—
Besides, they always smell of bread and butter.

LORD BYRON

One of life's unsolved mysteries
is what young girls giggle about.

E.C. McKenzie

Rebecca walked to school after the first morning. She loved this part of the day's programme. When the dew was not too heavy and the weather was fair there was a short cut through the woods. She turned off the main road, crept through uncle Josh Woodman's bars, waved away Mrs. Carter's cows, trod the short grass of the pasture, with its well-worn path running through gardens of buttercups and whiteweed, and groves of ivory leaves and sweet fern. She descended a little hill, jumped from stone to stone across a woodland brook, startling the drowsy frogs, who were always winking and blinking in the morning sun. Then came the "woodsy bit," with her feet pressing the slippery carpet of brown pine needles; the "woodsy bit" so full of dewy morning, surprises, — fungous growths of brilliant orange and crimson springing up around the stumps of dead trees, beautiful things born in a single night; and now and then the miracle of a little clump of waxen Indian pipes, seen just quickly enough to be saved from her careless tread. Then she climbed a stile, went through a grassy meadow, slid under another pair of bars, and came out into the road again, having gained nearly half a mile. How delicious it all was!

Kate Douglas Wiggin
Rebecca of Sunnybrook Farm

Accordingly, the good lady bundled up her darlings in woollen jackets and wadded sacks, and put comforters round their necks, and a pair of striped gaiters on each little pair of legs, and worsted mittens on their hands, and gave them a kiss apiece, by way of a spell to keep away Jack Frost. Forth sallied the two children, with a hop-skip-and-jump, that carried them at once into the very heart of a huge snow-drift, whence Violet emerged like a snow-bunting, while little Peony floundered out with his round face in full bloom. Then what a merry time had they! To look at them, frolicking in the wintry garden, you would have thought that the dark and pitiless storm had been sent for no other purpose but to provide a new plaything for Violet and Peony; and that they themselves had been created, as the snow-birds were, to take delight only in the tempest, and in the white mantle which it spread over the earth.

At last, when they had frosted one another all over with handfuls of snow, Violet, after laughing heartily at little Peony's figure, was struck with a new idea.

"You look exactly like a snow-image, Peony," said she, "if your cheeks were not so red. And that puts me in mind! Let us make an image out of snow,—an image of a little girl,—and it shall be our sister, and shall run about and play with us all winter long. Won't it be nice?"

"Oh yes!" cried Peony, as plainly as he could speak, for he was but a little boy. "That will be nice! And mamma shall see it!"

NATHANIEL HAWTHORNE
The Snow Image

44

There is that quiet in her face
That comes to all who toil.
She moves through all the sheaves with grace
A daughter of the soil.

There is that beauty in her hands,
That glory in her hair,
That adds a warmth to sun-brown lands
When Autumn cools the air.

There is that gladness in her eyes,
As one who finds the dust
A lovely path to Paradise,
And common things august.

There is that reverence in her mood,
That patience sweet and broad,
As one who in the solitude
Yet walks the fields with God!

EDWARD WILBUR MASON
"Ruth the Toiler"

Now blackberries were ripe, and in the hot afternoons Laura went with Ma to pick them. The big, black, juicy berries hung thick in brier patches in the creek bottoms. Some were in the shade of trees and some were in the sun, but the sun was so hot that Laura and Ma stayed in the shade. There were plenty of berries...Laura's fingers and her mouth were purple-black with berry juice. Her face and her hands and her bare feet were covered with brier scratches and mosquito bites. And they were spattered with purple stains, too, where she had slapped at the mosquitoes. But every day they brought home pails full of berries, and Ma spread them in the sun to dry.

LAURA INGALLS WILDER
Little House on the Prairie

Children know the grace of God
Better than most of us.
They see the world
The way the morning brings it
    back to them,
New and born and fresh and wonderful.

ARCHIBALD MACLEISH